MW01674826

Original title:
Artistic Intuition Unlocked

Author: Jessy Jänes
ISBN HARDBACK: 978-9916-87-837-8
ISBN PAPERBACK: 978-9916-87-838-5
ISBN EBOOK: 978-9916-87-839-2

The Pulse of the Universe

In the silence of the night,
Stars whisper to the dark.
Galaxies swirl and twirl,
Each a fleeting spark.

Time drifts like ocean waves,
Waves that kiss the shore.
Every heartbeat resonates,
In cosmic, ancient lore.

Nebulas bloom in colors bright,
Painting the vast void.
Life finds ways to shimmer,
In places once destroyed.

Planets dance in orbits grand,
A rhythm pure and true.
The pulse of life unending,
Connects me and you.

In the depths of blackened space,
Hope glimmers, bold and fierce.
Across the endless tapestry,
Our dreams, the stars will pierce.

Uncharted Artistic Realms

In the silence of a canvas,
Colors dance without a sound.
Each brushstroke builds a story,
In realms where dreams are found.

Shapes undulate like whispers,
Fragments of the mind's delight.
In uncharted artistic realms,
Life's vibrancy ignites the night.

Textures leap with eager hands,
Woven threads of time and space.
Imagination's wild flight,
Creates a wondrous place.

Hidden worlds behind the veil,
Where shadows play and secrets gleam.
Each corner holds a mystery,
A portal to a dream.

Through the eyes of ages past,
New visions take their bold stance.
In every hue and every brush,
There lies an endless dance.

Journey into the Abstract

Beneath the surface of the real,
Lies a landscape yet unknown.
A journey into the abstract,
Where colors freely roam.

Thoughts collide like rolling waves,
Merging in a vibrant storm.
In every twist and every turn,
New ideas take their form.

Shapes dissolve into the air,
Fleeting moments of pure grace.
Each fragment tells a truth uncut,
In this enchanted space.

With a heart wide open, we dive,
Into depths of painted dreams.
Where reason bends and time stands still,
And nothing's as it seems.

Shapes and colors intertwine,
Unraveling the mind's own skin.
This journey into the abstract,
Is where all life begins.

Illuminated Imaginings

In whispers soft and shadows bright,
Illuminated imaginings play.
A dance of thoughts upon the night,
Guiding lost souls who stray.

Each flicker tells a different tale,
Casting spells of vibrant glow.
In the caverns of our minds,
New wonders start to flow.

With every spark a journey blooms,
Across the canvas of the dark.
In colors rich as a thousand plumes,
We find our hidden spark.

These visions leap like fireflies,
Into realms where none have been.
Illuminated imaginings rise,
With every breath, serene.

A tapestry of dreams unfolds,
In this sacred, timeless space.
We hold the light that softly molds,
The boundaries of our grace.

The Nexus of Thought and Color

At the nexus of thought and color,
Ideas swirl in vibrant streams.
Where logic bends and passions flow,
Creating a tapestry of dreams.

Hues of blue and shades of gold,
Merge with whispers of the mind.
In this space, stories unfold,
Rich textures for hearts to find.

Each brushstroke sings a melody,
A symphony of sight and sound.
From chaos comes sweet harmony,
As new palettes dance around.

In every corner, thought ignites,
In spirals of kaleidoscope light.
We find connection in the art,
As day surrenders to the night.

This meeting place of heart and hue,
Holds worlds we've yet to see.
At the nexus of thought and color,
We become what we can be.

Fluid Boundaries

Waves crash upon the shore,
Bringing whispers from the deep.
Lines blurred where we explore,
Secrets that the oceans keep.

The sky meets water's face,
A dance of light and shade.
In this tender, vast space,
Nature's truths are laid.

Tides pull and tides release,
Each moment, a new start.
Finding in this fluid peace,
Interwoven, heart to heart.

Seas stretch beyond the seen,
Horizons call to roam.
In the spaces, we glean,
Our ever-changing home.

Boundaries fade like mist,
Embracing what's unknown.
In the swell, we coexist,
The journey, all our own.

The Song of Expression

A melody begins to rise,
Carried on the breath of dreams.
Words dance beneath the skies,
Flowing like sunlight beams.

Colors splash across the page,
Each stroke tells a story true.
In the silence of the stage,
Voices find the light to break through.

Expressions born from the soul,
Crafted with both love and pain.
In the echoes, we feel whole,
A harmony we gain.

Notes linger in the air,
A chorus of hearts combined.
In creation, we all share,
The essence of mankind.

Tune your heart to the sound,
Feel the rhythm deep inside.
In this song, we are found,
Together we will glide.

Nature’s Quiet Muse

Beneath the boughs, whispers call,
Leaves rustle like soft sighs.
In this haven, I feel small,
Yet my spirit learns to rise.

Morning dew on blades of grass,
Glitters in the warming light.
Time, in moments, moves so fast,
Yet nature holds me tight.

Mountains loom with wisdom old,
Guardians of this sacred space.
In their shadows, I feel bold,
Finding strength in their embrace.

Streams hum softly with delight,
Carving paths through stone and earth.
In their flow, I find my light,
Rebirth from nature's birth.

In quiet, lessons abide,
Simple truths of what is real.
In this stillness, I confide,
Finding peace in each reveal.

Crafting Dreams in Silence

In the hush of night's embrace,
Ideas flutter like soft wings.
Here, creativity finds its place,
In the quiet, silence sings.

Thoughts emerge like stars aglow,
Illuminating hidden paths.
In this calm, seeds of vision sow,
Hopes thrive in the aftermath.

With every breath, a promise grows,
Nurtured by the moon's soft light.
In the shadows, inspiration flows,
Drawing dreams to take flight.

Silence carries wisdom deep,
Where the noise of day fades slow.
In this refuge, secrets keep,
Fostering the dreams we sow.

Crafted gently, visions weave,
A tapestry of what may be.
In this silence, we believe,
Boundless worlds for us to see.

Painting with Shadows

In the twilight's soft embrace,
Shadows dance with gentle grace.
Colors meld, a muted play,
Night reveals what dreams convey.

Brushstrokes whisper tales untold,
In hues of amber, blush, and gold.
Canvas breathes, alive and free,
A world born from mystery.

Darkness cradles light's retreat,
Where silence wraps, and echoes meet.
From the depths, visions arise,
Painting truth that never lies.

A palette rich in longing sighs,
While moonlight weaves through starry skies.
In shadows deep, dreams intertwine,
Crafting art, both yours and mine.

The Breath of Inspiration

Inhale the whispers of the breeze,
Exhale the burdens, set them free.
A dance of thoughts begins to flow,
In stillness, seeds of wonder grow.

The spark ignites, a flame so bright,
Illuminating the darkest night.
Ideas pulse, like veins in sync,
In every pause, in every blink.

Nature's canvas, a vivid muse,
Colors swirl, and paths confuse.
Yet in chaos, clarity blooms,
Awakening hearts from endless glooms.

Let the rhythm guide your hand,
Crafting dreams, both bold and grand.
Each breath a step, a journey vast,
In fleeting moments, hold them fast.

Sculpting Thoughts

In the quiet of the mind's expanse,
Clay of ideas waits for a chance.
Hands of time mold every dream,
Sculpting visions with every seam.

Chiseling edges, refining line,
From raw emotion, shapes intertwine.
With every touch, the essence grows,
A masterpiece, as passion flows.

Impressions linger, soft and bold,
Stories of life and tales untold.
In every curve, a voice is found,
Resonating through the ground.

Crafting futures from the past,
An artist’s heart beats deep and fast.
Like marble forged from starlit dust,
In creation, we place our trust.

Celestial Whispers

Beneath the canvas of the night,
Stars weave stories, pure and bright.
Whispers dance on cosmic tides,
In the vastness, where hope abides.

Comets trace their silver trails,
Each one holding a thousand tales.
Galaxies spin, a wondrous waltz,
In their beauty, our hearts convulse.

Nebulas bloom in splashes bold,
Cradling secrets, shimmered gold.
The universe sings soft and low,
In its rhythm, our spirits flow.

With every heartbeat, we unite,
In the silence, we feel the light.
Celestial dreams adorn the skies,
In their embrace, our essence flies.

Tapestries of Emotion

Threads of joy weave tight,
In shadows whispers dance,
A tapestry of light,
With every fleeting glance.

Colors blend and fade,
Stories told in seams,
Through tears and laughter laid,
We stitch our silent dreams.

Woven hearts entwine,
Patterns rich and bold,
Each fiber a design,
In stories yet untold.

Beneath the surface lies,
A world of hidden fears,
In woven whispers cry,
The threads of hopes and tears.

With every thread and knot,
A journey to embrace,
In this tapestry, we're caught,
A warm, familiar space.

A Symphony of Shapes

Circles spin with grace,
Triangles stand so tall,
In this vibrant place,
Squares form a steady wall.

Lines that dance and sway,
Curves that gently bend,
Shapes that guide the way,
As colors intertwine and blend.

Geometry's delight,
Crafted with pure care,
A symphony takes flight,
In the open air.

Each form tells a story,
Of beauty in design,
In every shape and glory,
A realm where we align.

Together they create,
A harmony so sweet,
In this grand estate,
Where shapes and rhythms meet.

Hidden Landscapes

Beneath the surface waits,
A world both lush and rare,
Where silence celebrates,
The secrets held with care.

Mountains cloaked in mist,
Rivers softly flow,
In the quiet, persist,
The tales that nature knows.

Valleys rich with dreams,
Wonders to behold,
In sunlight’s golden beams,
Whispers yet untold.

Caves that breathe with time,
Echoes of the past,
In this hidden rhyme,
Freedom's shadows cast.

Every step reveals,
A treasure yet unseen,
In these landscapes’ reels,
Life’s vivid tapestry green.

The Fire of Inspiration

Flickering embers glow,
In the heart of the night,
A spark begins to grow,
Igniting the inner light.

Winds of change may blow,
Fueling the fierce flame,
Inspiration’s flow,
Illuminating the name.

With every burning thought,
Ideas leap and soar,
From ashes, all is brought,
To create and to explore.

In the silence, it thrives,
A dance of passion's flare,
Where creativity strives,
Beyond the mundane care.

And as the fire burns,
A warmth that’s felt by all,
In every heart, it turns,
To answer the calling’s call.

The Journey of a Thousand Strokes

With brush in hand, I start my quest,
Each stroke a step, a silent test.
Colors blend in harmony,
A canvas waits for destiny.

The path is long, yet joys unfold,
In shadows deep, and stories told.
Every mark a whispering tale,
A voyage where dreams shall sail.

Through highs and lows, I learn to see,
The beauty lies in all that be.
With every layer, truths emerge,
My heart ignites, I feel the surge.

As worlds take shape, the time will pass,
A tapestry of moments vast.
In each creation, I find my part,
The light and dark entwine the heart.

So here I stand, brush poised to write,
A journey painted in pure light.
With every stroke, a story grows,
In art, my spirit forever flows.

Serendipity in Art

Brush meets canvas, fate aligns,
Accidental strokes, beauty shines.
A splash of color, intention bends,
In chaos, charm gracefully blends.

Moments found in the silent space,
Where art transforms a fleeting face.
A glance, a spark, a muse may come,
In randomness, the heart beats drum.

Through tangled thoughts, a vision clear,
Unexpected joys, I hold them near.
Each quirk and flaw a story spins,
In serendipity, magic begins.

Layers build in forgotten time,
The unplanned path, a secret rhyme.
To weave such wonder, let it flow,
In art's embrace, let spirits glow.

So here I dwell, in chance's grace,
Finding beauty in every trace.
A journey blessed, unfurling heart,
In life's wild dance, we find our art.

The Unfurled Imagination

A spark ignites, the mind takes flight,
In realms unseen, beyond the night.
With wings unfurled, I dare to dream,
In colors bright, my thoughts agleam.

Ideas bloom like flowers bright,
In garden rich, pure delight.
Through whispered winds, I hear their call,
Imagination's dance, enthralling all.

Each vision blooms, a world I trace,
With open heart, I find my place.
The canvas waits, my spirit soars,
In every brushstroke, adventure pours.

In realms of wonder, I shall dwell,
Where stories weave and passions swell.
To push the limits, break the mold,
In dreams untold, my heart turns bold.

So let me wander, explore, create,
In every heartbeat, the threads of fate.
The unfurled mind, a graceful art,
Embracing all, the wild heart.

Visions That Speak

In colors bright, the silence sings,
A canvas whispers, the heart takes wings.
Each hue a story, a truth that's felt,
Visions formed where emotions dwelt.

Through vibrant strokes, the soul ignites,
In shapes and forms, the spirit writes.
A dialogue shared between the lines,
In every piece, a glimpse, it finds.

As shadows dance and light reveals,
The essence of what art conceals.
A world unfolds, in stillness deep,
Visions that speak, their promises keep.

In every glance, a truth emerges,
An echo of life, the heart converges.
Each piece a bond, a silent creed,
In the artistry, we find the seed.

With every brush, a heart laid bare,
In these creations, love and care.
Visions that speak, a language pure,
In art's embrace, our souls endure.

The Symphony of the Unseen

In shadows dance the whispers low,
A melody that few can know.
The stars align in silent grace,
Composing dreams in endless space.

Beneath the moon's soft silver light,
Echoes soar beyond the night.
Invisible hands weave thoughts so bright,
A symphony of pure delight.

Time flows like water in a stream,
Moments crafted from a dream.
Notes unseen play in the air,
Each heartbeat sings a secret prayer.

In the quiet, sounds collide,
Feelings bloom where fears reside.
Harmony in stillness found,
The unseen world, a sacred sound.

So listen close, let silence reign,
The symphony will ease your pain.
Embrace the chords of what is true,
An unseen dance, just me and you.

Ways of the Heart

In whispers soft, the heart does speak,
A path of love, both bold and meek.
Each beat a tale of joys and scars,
Mapping dreams to distant stars.

The winding roads, they twist and turn,
With every step, new lessons learn.
In laughter shared and tears that fall,
The heart's true language conquers all.

Moments linger in the air,
A gentle touch, a knowing stare.
Through storms faced and sunlit days,
We navigate love's endless maze.

Compassion flows like rivers wide,
Holding secrets that we confide.
Embrace the ways that love imparts,
For every journey starts with hearts.

With every pulse, a story flows,
In quiet times, the heart bestows.
Trust the paths that feel like home,
For in these ways, we are never alone.

Meditations in Color

Splash of red ignites the soul,
A vibrant hue to make us whole.
In quiet thought, the colors play,
With each brushstroke, dreams convey.

Blue waves roll on tranquil shores,
Whispers of peace behind closed doors.
In depth of hues, reflections find,
A canvas where the heart unwinds.

Golden rays in morning light,
Awakening the world so bright.
Textures blend, creating space,
For silent thoughts we dare embrace.

In shades of green, the life unfolds,
A tapestry of stories told.
Nature's voice, in colors deep,
Invites our souls to wake from sleep.

Let colors dance upon your mind,
In every hue, life's truths unwind.
Meditate in shades, explore,
And find the beauty at your core.

Chords of Creation

From silence born, the music swells,
In every note, a story tells.
Creation sings in vibrant sound,
In harmony, the world is found.

With gentle strums and rhythms bold,
The fabric of the universe unfolds.
Melodies that stitch the seams,
Of every heart and all its dreams.

In every chord, an echo lives,
A testament to what love gives.
With every beat, life finds its way,
Creating magic day by day.

Potent force in every key,
Awakening what's yet to be.
In symphonies both grand and small,
The chords of life unite us all.

So let your spirit join the song,
In creation's dance, we all belong.
With hands entwined, let's celebrate,
The chords of life that resonate.

Ephemeral Visions

Whispers in the wind, soft and light,
Fleeting moments dance, out of sight.
Colors blend in twilight's embrace,
Dreams take flight, a soft trace.

Glimmers fade with the break of day,
Memories linger, then drift away.
Captured in hearts, yet hard to hold,
Stories written in threads of gold.

In silence, shadows gently weave,
A tapestry of hope, we believe.
Fragile as breath, yet strong in song,
Life's fleeting beauty, where we belong.

Echoes of laughter, soft and sweet,
Moments of joy, time's heartbeat.
A glance, a smile, all ephemeral,
Building worlds, now ethereal.

Though visions fade, they leave a mark,
In the depths of night, a spark.
Ephemeral dreams, they linger near,
Carried by whispers for all to hear.

From Chaos Comes Clarity

In the storm's eye, silence reigns,
Fury subsides, clarity gains.
Amid the tangle, threads unwind,
Answers emerge, the heart aligned.

Colors of chaos, vibrant and bold,
Hidden truths, waiting to be told.
A spark of light cuts through the grey,
Guiding souls to a brighter way.

From the pandemonium arises peace,
Life's intricacies find their release.
Through the tumult, visions unfold,
Moments of wisdom in stories told.

Each challenge faced becomes a guide,
In chaos, strength we cannot hide.
Lessons in shadows, wisdom in tears,
Transforming pain into brighter years.

So let the winds of chaos blow,
Amidst the turmoil, we learn and grow.
From storms of life, clarity gleams,
Emerging from darkness, we embrace our dreams.

Dreamweaver's Palette

Colors swirl on a canvas bright,
Brushstrokes dance in the moonlight.
Whispers of dreams, vivid and free,
Crafting worlds for hearts to see.

Twilight paints with hues divine,
Imaginations blend, intertwine.
In silence, visions come alive,
A palette where all dreams thrive.

Echoes of stardust in each hue,
Artistry of life, ever new.
Brush of the heart, strokes of the mind,
Creating magic, one of a kind.

Through the colors, emotions flow,
In every shade, a tale to show.
Dreams take shape with every line,
In the artist's heart, all shines fine.

So let us paint with fearless hearts,
Dreaming and weaving as life imparts.
On the canvas of night, we will play,
Unleashing visions in bright array.

Threads of Velvet Sound

Whispers of music fill the air,
Gentle notes, beyond compare.
Each chord strummed, a story weaves,
Voices rise like autumn leaves.

A melody flows, silky and warm,
Wrapping souls in a soothing calm.
Harmony dances, intertwines,
Crafting a world where light shines.

In echoes soft, memories cling,
Notes linger long, as hearts take wing.
Rhythms pulse in quiet nights,
Life's serenade, our shared delights.

Threads of sound, both bold and sweet,
Each heartbeat found in its retreat.
Melodies linger, a gentle embrace,
A tapestry of time and space.

With every note, a dream unfolds,
In velvet threads, our story's told.
So let the music lead us round,
In the embrace of velvet sound.

Kaleidoscope of Dreams

In twilight's embrace, colors blend,
Whispers of wishes that never end.
A canvas of thoughts, vibrant and bright,
Guiding the soul through the deep of night.

Mirrors reflecting the dance of fate,
Patterns unfold, never hesitate.
Each turn reveals a story anew,
A kaleidoscope spins, dreams break through.

Moments like petals in springtime bloom,
Filling the heart with fragrant perfume.
Life's tapestry woven with care,
In shades of wonder, floating in air.

From shadows to light, a glorious shift,
Every heartbeat, a precious gift.
In the mind’s eye, adventures take flight,
Kaleidoscope visions, pure and white.

So wander in dreams, let your heart soar,
In colors unseen, forever explore.
The journey of life, a grand parade,
In the tapestry of dreams, never fade.

The Key to Inspired Hearts

In the silence of dawn, a whisper appears,
Unlocking the dreams that dwell through the years.
A gentle reminder, passion ignites,
The key to the heart in magical flights.

Creativity dances on soft, painted wings,
Each note a treasure, the silence sings.
Moments of genius, bright as a star,
Illuminating paths, guiding from afar.

With every heartbeat, inspiration flows,
The canvas of life, where nothing is froze.
Imagination's spark, glowing so bright,
Guiding our spirits toward endless light.

So treasure the moments that make you feel,
The key to your heart, let it reveal.
The power of dreams, let them entwine,
In the symphony of life, feel divine.

Unlock the wonders that lie deep inside,
With a heart full of courage, let love be your guide.
Inspiring the world with the truth of your art,
Find the connection, the key to each heart.

Secrets of the Creative Flame

In the shadows, a flicker lies,
Whispering secrets beneath the skies.
A flame that dances, bold and bright,
Igniting the spark, chasing the night.

Canvas awaits, the brush in hand,
Colors like whispers, an artist's band.
Every stroke sings a tale untold,
The secrets emerge, as dreams unfold.

From ashes of doubt, brilliance is born,
In the quiet of chaos, the heart's adorned.
Creativity flows like rivers wide,
A treasure chest deep where wonders abide.

So gather the spark and let it ignite,
Hold tight to the dreams that feel just right.
In the fire's glow, find peace and grace,
With secrets of passion, embrace your place.

The creative flame, a guide divine,
In the depths of your soul, forever shine.
Let the world see what dances within,
Embrace your artistry; let it begin.

Flight of Fancy

A delicate breeze carries dreams untold,
Stories of hearts, both timid and bold.
Wings of imagination take to the sky,
In a world of wonder, we learn to fly.

Clouds of cotton, fluffy and white,
Where wishes drift softly, out of sight.
Dancing through realms of whimsical grace,
In the heart of a dream, we find our place.

With laughter like echoes of joyful delight,
We chase the horizon, from morning to night.
Every heartbeat a rhythm, a melody sweet,
In the dance of the aether, our spirits meet.

So lift up your gaze and embrace the flight,
For the sky is a canvas, bathed in pure light.
In the journey of dreams, let your spirit roam,
In the flight of fancy, we find our home.

Together we wander through valleys of air,
Embracing the magic that's hidden with care.
With wings made of courage, we soar and we laugh,
In the flight of fancy, find your true path.

Heartbeats on Canvas

Brushstroke whispers in the night,
Colors dance in merging light.
Each heartbeat paints a tale untold,
In every hue, emotions bold.

Canvas breathes beneath my hands,
Stories spun like golden sands.
With every stroke, the dream ignites,
A world reborn in vibrant sights.

Silent echoes, shades collide,
Where feelings dwell and fears reside.
The artist's heart, a fragile thing,
In every line, a song to sing.

Capturing souls in fleeting time,
Evoking love, evoking crime.
The masterpiece, a mirror drawn,
Reflects the dusk, embraces dawn.

So let the canvas breathe anew,
As heartbeats dance in vibrant hue.
With every touch, the spirit glows,
In swirls of passion that the painter knows.

When Dreams Take Shape

In the quiet dawn, hope awakes,
Whispers of change, the heart aches.
Dreams like shadows stretch and sway,
Guiding the lost along the way.

Sketching futures in the air,
Imagination, free and rare.
Colors blend, desires rise,
In the canvas of the skies.

When visions merge, possibilities bloom,
Each fragment dispels the looming gloom.
Rise, my spirit, take the flight,
Transform the dark, embrace the light.

Let passion flow without restrain,
Chasing whispers, dancing in the rain.
With every hour, the dream unfolds,
In the heart, a tale it holds.

So chase the stars, let courage steer,
The path revealed when dreams are near.
With each step, the vision's clear,
In the embrace of hopes sincere.

Echoes of the Unseen

In silent woods, the whispers dwell,
Echoes weave a secret spell.
Nature's heart beats soft and slow,
While mysteries in shadows grow.

Footsteps hush on the forest floor,
Stories linger, tales of yore.
Each rustle speaks of what we've missed,
In fleeting moments, dreams persist.

The unseen world dances in light,
Chasing shadows, taking flight.
A symphony of life unfolds,
In every leaf, a secret holds.

The wind carries notes from afar,
Guiding lost souls with its gentle star.
In every sigh, each breath we take,
Nature's pulse, a bond we wake.

Embrace the whispers, feel the grace,
Find solace in this hidden place.
For in the echoes, truth we find,
A gentle call that unites the mind.

The Surge of Imagination

Within the mind, a tempest brews,
Ideas dance in vibrant hues.
A spark ignites, the vision's clear,
Imagination thrives, drawing near.

From depths of thought, the images rise,
Crafting worlds under endless skies.
A river flows with fervent grace,
Taking shape in time and space.

Dreams transform with gentle ease,
Like autumn leaves in playful breeze.
Freedom calls, no chains can bind,
In the realm where hearts unwind.

Creation sings, a symphonic roar,
Chasing shadows, seeking more.
With every brush, each word we speak,
The universe reveals its peak.

So let the surge of thought cascade,
Through valleys deep, in light and shade.
For in this dance, we come alive,
And breathe as one, our dreams to thrive.

The Canvas within

Colors swirl in silent grace,
Each thought a stroke, a sacred space.
Dreams unfold, like petals wide,
In this realm where spirits bide.

Emotions dance, a vivid hue,
Crafting worlds both old and new.
Whispers linger, soft and warm,
Nurtured in the heart's own charm.

Layers deep, they intertwine,
Stories hidden, yet they shine.
Every shade, a tale of past,
Boundless echoes, deep and vast.

Brush of time on life’s own screen,
Capture moments, felt, unseen.
A masterpiece that changes form,
A journey through the hidden storm.

In this space, I find my voice,
Amidst the chaos, I rejoice.
The canvas speaks, revealing true,
A world awaits within the view.

Tethered to the Infinite

Stars collide in endless night,
Gravity pulls, a silent flight.
Hope reaches out, a fragile thread,
Binding dreams that dance ahead.

In the vastness, shadows play,
Guiding whispers lead the way.
Time drifts on, a gentle stream,
Caught between the now and dream.

Open hearts can brave the void,
Bridge the gap, the fear destroyed.
Unseen forces pull us close,
Together, we dare to propose.

Through the darkness, we will rise,
Beneath the cloak of endless skies.
Hands entwined, we find our path,
Tethered souls, we forge our math.

Infinite realms, our spirits soar,
Journeying far, evermore.
With every heartbeat, we chase light,
Entwined in love, we take our flight.

Murmurs of the Subconscious

In whispers soft, the shadows breathe,
Thoughts entwined, like webs they weave.
Secrets buried, buried deep,
In the corners, where dreamers sleep.

Fleeting images swirl and fade,
Echoes of the choices made.
Fears and hopes, they intertwine,
In the labyrinths of the mind.

A flicker here, a fleeting glance,
Lost in the hypnotic trance.
Voices murmur, calling clear,
A dance of past, a song of fear.

In these depths, the truth reveals,
Crimson petals, aching feels.
Through the fog, light starts to gleam,
Awakening the hidden dream.

Embrace the chaos, let it flow,
In the silence, seeds will grow.
Murmurs guide us through it all,
Into the depths, we rise, we fall.

Mosaic of the Mind

Fragments scattered on the floor,
Each a glimpse, a closing door.
Memories crafted, shapes confined,
A tapestry of the mind.

Broken pieces, sharp and bright,
Colorful shards reflect the light.
In the chaos, patterns seek,
Silent whispers softly speak.

Thoughts collide in vivid dreams,
A dance of shadow, light, and beams.
Hues of passion, fears combined,
Creating art, the soul aligned.

In this mosaic, stories blend,
A journey that will never end.
United fragments, strong yet frail,
Life's rich fabric tells the tale.

With each glance, a new view shared,
Within the chaos, beauty spared.
Mosaic whispers to the heart,
In every piece, we play a part.

Surrendering to the Flow

In rivers where the waters dive,
I find the pulse of life alive.
The gentle push, the soft caress,
I let go, embracing rest.

The currents wrap around my soul,
A whispered truth, a quiet goal.
With every wave, I lose my fear,
For in the flow, I draw you near.

The past drifts softly like the breeze,
A dance of leaves among the trees.
Each moment shared, a sacred trust,
Letting go is more than just.

In stillness found beneath the roar,
I breathe in deep and crave for more.
The world unravels, becomes clear,
In sacred silence, you are here.

With open arms, I greet the tide,
Where dreams and hopes do now reside.
I flow with life, a cosmic thread,
Surrendering to love instead.

The Secret Language of Forms

Shapes appear in shadows cast,
Whispers held in moments past.
Lines connect and curves embrace,
Architecture of time and space.

In patterns bold, the stories weave,
A tapestry we can believe.
Each angle speaks, each depth reveals,
The truth concealed that the heart feels.

Geometry of dreams undone,
In the dance of sun and fun.
Figures twirl in silent grace,
Inviting us to find our place.

The language speaks in forms alive,
Where thoughts can play and visions thrive.
Unraveled in the artist's hands,
A universe of love expands.

In every line, a message hides,
In every curve, the heart abides.
Listen close, the secrets told,
In shapes and shadows, we behold.

Subtle Currents of Discovery

In quiet moments, thoughts arise,
A gentle flow beneath the skies.
Each question lingers, softly spun,
Revealing paths where dreams begun.

The subtle pull, the hidden clues,
In every choice, the heart can muse.
With every step, new worlds appear,
In pathways drawn, I lose my fear.

The treasure lies in whispered winds,
Where nature sings and gently spins.
I wander through these sacred halls,
Here in the stillness, magic calls.

Each ripple holds a memory sweet,
In quietude, my pulse and beat.
The currents guide, they shape my way,
Leading me to the break of day.

Understanding blooms like spring's first light,
In tender moments, truth takes flight.
With open heart, I choose to see,
The lovely dance of mystery.

Portraits of Hope

Through stained glass beams, the colors play,
Illuminating dreams today.
Each portrait shines with stories bold,
In every heart, a dream retold.

The brushstrokes weave a tapestry,
Of love and loss, of you and me.
In vibrant hues, the future glows,
A canvas rich with highs and lows.

Eyes that sparkle, hearts that soar,
With every gaze, hope opens doors.
We paint our paths with colors bright,
Embracing shadows, sharing light.

Together, we frame the life we crave,
Standing tall, unafraid, brave.
In portraits drawn with tender care,
We capture dreams suspended in air.

Each face a story, each smile a spark,
A celebration in love's park.
With every stroke, our spirits blend,
In portraits of hope that never end.

Whispers of the Muse

In the stillness of night, she sighs,
Echoes dance under starry skies.
Thoughts untangle, like threads of light,
Guiding the heart to take flight.

Words weave softly, a gentle flow,
Inspiration blooms where shadows grow.
A canvas waits, so pure and bare,
Waiting for dreams to find their air.

Melodies linger, sweet and low,
In every whisper, a world to sow.
Brush in hand, the heart's delight,
With colors bright, the soul takes flight.

Figures leap from obscured depths,
Each stroke a promise, stolen breaths.
A symphony of sight and sound,
In every moment, connection found.

Through the chaos, a path appears,
Freed from doubt, embraced by cheers.
In the quiet, her song we trace,
The whispers of the muse embrace.

Colors Beyond the Veil

Beneath the surface, hues collide,
A tapestry of dreams, side by side.
Shades of laughter, breaths of pain,
Whispered secrets fall like rain.

Every stroke, a story told,
In vibrant splashes, brave and bold.
Glimmers of hope in a world so wide,
Colorful shadows on a radiant ride.

The sun dips low, igniting the skies,
Painting the evening with whispered cries.
Mystic colors weave through the air,
An artist's vision, beyond compare.

In every twist, a journey flows,
Life's complexities in vibrant shows.
Behind the veil, we seek and find,
A spectrum of hearts, beautifully aligned.

With every brush, horizons shift,
From darkness into light, a gifted lift.
Colors arise, wild and free,
Beyond the veil, we learn to see.

The Hidden Palette

In quiet corners, secrets keep,
A hidden palette, memories seep.
Layered whispers, rich and deep,
Where shadows linger, dreams dare leap.

Painted sighs of days gone by,
Echoes of laughter that softly cry.
Each hue a moment, vibrant true,
A glimpse of life in every hue.

From muted tones to bursts of light,
Canvas awakens, heart takes flight.
Textures meld, the past unfolds,
In every stroke, a story holds.

Through tangled paths of thought and time,
Emotions braiding in gentle rhyme.
A symphony of sights and sounds,
In this hidden place, beauty abounds.

As shadows shift and colors blend,
The hidden palette learns to mend.
With brush in hand, the soul takes hold,
Creating life in hues of gold.

Brushstrokes of the Soul

With every stroke, emotions bloom,
Brushstrokes of the soul, dispelling gloom.
A canvas vast, a heart laid bare,
Color and light, a tender affair.

Each layer tells of joys and fears,
Whispered memories, silent tears.
As pigments dance and shadows play,
The essence of life in bright display.

Moments captured, time suspended,
Through a glance, our spirits blended.
Artistry flows as feelings swell,
In this quiet space, we dwell.

A fusion deep, our stories merge,
In every line, the passions surge.
For in creation, we discover,
The brushstrokes of the soul uncover.

Embrace the chaos, embrace the calm,
In vibrant colors, find the balm.
With brush in hand, let silence speak,
In timeless realms, our dreams we seek.

The Beneath of Every Scene

In shadows deep, secrets abide,
Whispers entwined, where dreams collide.
The truth unfolds in silent grace,
Beneath the veil, we find our place.

A canvas drawn with unseen shades,
Life's tapestry, where hope cascades.
In quiet corners, stories dwell,
Unraveled threads, all hearts can tell.

The echoes of laughter linger long,
In every heartbreak, a healing song.
Time weaves strands, both tight and loose,
In every loss, we find our truth.

Beyond the surface, beauty lies,
In every tear, a soft disguise.
Among the layers, we shall roam,
To find within, a sacred home.

So cast your gaze on what is near,
The depths of life, both brave and clear.
In every scene, the heart will glean,
The stories told, the love unseen.

The Light Between Heartbeats

Moments pause in tender sighs,
A fleeting glance, a whispered prize.
In stillness found, we often wait,
For glimmers bright to conflate.

Each heartbeat echoes life's sweet song,
In the intervals, we belong.
With every breath, the world aligns,
A dance of souls, where fate intertwines.

Between the beats, there's space to feel,
A quiet pulse, both soft and real.
The light that breaks in silent ways,
Guides us through the shadowed days.

Time stretches thin, then draws us close,
In every heartbeat, love's sweet dose.
For in this rhythm, life's embrace,
The light we seek finds its place.

So hold your breath and close your eyes,
And feel the magic that underlies.
In those brief beats, our spirits soar,
Illuminating paths to explore.

Shattered Boundaries

Walls that confine, we dare to break,
With every step, new paths we make.
Beyond the limits, dreams take flight,
In shattered pieces, we find our light.

Each fracture tells a tale untold,
Of courage found, of hearts so bold.
In chaos, beauty starts to bloom,
From broken shards, we weave our loom.

The chains of doubt begin to rust,
As hope ignites with quiet trust.
Together we rise, hand in hand,
Beyond the borders, we make our stand.

No longer confined by fear or shame,
We dance upon the shards of pain.
In unity's strength, we find our way,
Through shattered dreams, we greet the day.

So let the world see us ascend,
From brokenness, we will not bend.
In every crack, a story thrives,
As shattered boundaries spark new lives.

Riding the Waves of Thought

Thoughts like ocean tides will flow,
With every rise, a gentle glow.
In depths of mind, the currents sway,
We navigate, come what may.

On crests of ideas, we fly so high,
Drifting freely, like clouds in the sky.
Each wave a glimpse of what could be,
A journey forged through the vast sea.

In storms of doubt, we may be tossed,
Yet in the chaos, we find what's lost.
The rhythm guides our hearts to shore,
In every wave, we seek for more.

With sails unfurled, we chase the breeze,
Through whispers of dreams, we ride with ease.
On waves of thought, our spirits dance,
Embracing life, we take the chance.

So let us ride the tides of fate,
In every moment, we create.
Among the waves, we'll find our truth,
In endless seas, we reclaim our youth.

Ethereal Echoes

Whispers drift on twilight air,
Softly spoken, secrets shared.
In the silence, shadows play,
Echoing the light of day.

Stars awaken, watch and gleam,
Fleeting glimpses of a dream.
Ghostly murmurs fill the night,
Carrying the lost in flight.

Moonlit paths begin to glow,
Guiding hearts where spirits flow.
In the stillness, truths entwine,
Ethereal threads, divine design.

Each soul’s voice, a tale to tell,
Resonating like a bell.
In the echoes, we find peace,
As the whispers never cease.

Crimson dawn transforms the scene,
Fleeting thoughts, like drifting dream.
Ethereal echoes softly fade,
In the light, they’re gently laid.

Vivid Daydreams

Colors burst in painted skies,
Where the sweet imagination lies.
Floating visions in the breeze,
Dancing gently among the trees.

Waves of laughter, soft and bright,
Fragrant blossoms, pure delight.
In a world that's wrapped in haze,
Sun-kissed moments, endless days.

Every heartbeat's like a song,
Pulling us to where we belong.
In the canvas of our minds,
Vivid daydreams, joy behind.

Each brushstroke tells a story rare,
Tales of wonder floating in air.
In between the quiet sighs,
Reality and dreams arise.

Through the spiral of our thoughts,
Magic lives, and time is caught.
Vivid daydreams weave a spell,
In their world, we long to dwell.

Reflective Flows

Ripples dance on mirrored streams,
Carrying the weight of dreams.
In reflections, truths reveal,
Echoes of the heart we feel.

Nature whispers soft and clear,
Inviting peace to draw near.
Thoughts like petals drift and glide,
In the flow, our fears subside.

With each wave, the past unfolds,
Stories of the brave and bold.
In the current, time stands still,
Reflective beauty, gentle thrill.

Emotions wash like evening tide,
Carrying the hopes we hide.
Letting go, we breathe anew,
In the flow, our spirits grew.

Underneath the surface, deep,
Lies the wisdom we all keep.
In reflective flows, we find,
A river's heart, our soul entwined.

Mists of Creativity

Veils of fog, a quiet space,
Where ideas find their place.
In the ether, thoughts collide,
Mists of creativity abide.

Beneath the shroud of gentle night,
Sparkling visions take their flight.
Imagination, free and bold,
Crafting narratives untold.

In the stillness, whispers churn,
Flames of passion brightly burn.
Words weaved in a tapestry,
Fleeting glimpses, sets us free.

Brush and pen, our sacred tools,
Challenging the fickle rules.
Together, we create a dream,
In the mists where visions teem.

Wisdom lingers in the air,
Carving paths, both rare and fair.
Mists of creativity call,
Inviting us to risk it all.

Unraveled Threads of Thought

Whispers of wisdom drift and sway,
In shadows where lost memories play.
Each thread a story, a silent song,
Tangled in webs where they belong.

Blue skies murmur deep and low,
Through cracks of dawn, the light will flow.
Thoughts flutter, like leaves in flight,
Glimmers of truth in the fading night.

Hearts ponder paths, both old and new,
With questions cloaked in morning dew.
Journey unfolds with every breath,
In the space between life and death.

Gentle echoes ripple through time,
Lifting spirits with every rhyme.
From doubt to clarity, shadows clear,
The tapestry of thought draws near.

In silence found, the answers bloom,
Illuminating the darkest room.
As threads unravel, insights ignite,
Weaving brilliance into the light.

Enchanted Realms of Creation

In gardens where wild dreams reside,
Imagination soars like a tide.
Colors collide in a vibrant dance,
Inviting souls to take a chance.

Each brushstroke sings of worlds unknown,
In realms where seeds of wonder are sown.
With every hue, magic unfurls,
Creating dimension in hidden swirls.

Muses whisper secrets on the breeze,
In symphonies sung through rustling leaves.
Crafting tales as stars begin to twinkle,
In twilight's embrace, thoughts interlink.

Foundations built on dreams and light,
In sanctuaries where spirits take flight.
Each heartbeat echoes in moments rare,
An awakening, vibrant and fair.

Wonders bloom in the depths of the soul,
Creating a canvas where all feels whole.
In these enchanted realms, we play,
From the heart's whispers, we find our way.

Dreams on Canvas

A brush in hand, the world unfolds,
Colors whisper, stories retold.
Each stroke a wish upon the night,
Dreams emerge in radiant light.

Soft pastels blend with shadows deep,
A timeless tale that the heart will keep.
Canvas breathes, alive with intent,
In every corner, love is spent.

Figures dance in an unspoken trance,
Lost in the rhythm, lost in the chance.
Impressions linger, shadows align,
In vivid scenes where spirits entwine.

From chaos arises a beautiful hue,
With every drop, a dream comes true.
Visions burst forth, wild and free,
A reflection of who we can be.

Artistry sings of life’s sweet embrace,
In strokes of fortune, we find our place.
Dreams on canvas, forever they soar,
A testament to what we adore.

The Alchemy of Expression

Words like gold, turning lead to flight,
In the depths of the soul, shining bright.
Crafting magic from silence and sound,
Transforming hearts in moments profound.

Thoughts ignite, a brilliant spark,
Lighting pathways from dusk to dark.
Expressions flow like rivers wide,
Carving canyons where secrets hide.

Articulating dreams, untold and raw,
Resonating with truth, an unbroken law.
Emotions weave, a fabric divine,
Binding us together, yours and mine.

In vulnerability, courage stands,
Breaking barriers, reaching out hands.
Transcending limits with every line,
Alchemy transforms the mundane to divine.

Through whispers, shouts, and everything in between,
The essence of life, rich and serene.
The alchemy of expression unfolds,
In every heartbeat, a story retold.

Brushstrokes of Inspiration

With each stroke, the canvas sings,
A tale of dreams and vibrant flings.
Colors swirl in a dance divine,
Brush in hand, the world is mine.

Secrets hidden in shades of night,
Whispers of dawn in morning light.
A palette rich, so full, so bright,
Every hue holds a soul's delight.

Moments captured, time stands still,
Each line a thought, each shape a will.
In every curve, a story flows,
A journey forged where passion grows.

With fervent heart, the artist breathes,
As dreams take flight on vivid sheaths.
Inspiration dances, wild and free,
In every brushstroke, eternity.

The canvas waits, a silent plea,
To capture life in shades of glee.
In the end, it tells our truth,
A timeless tale, the spirit's youth.

Whispers of the Muse

In the stillness, a voice does call,
Softly weaving beneath the thrall.
An echo sweet, of dreams untold,
In shadows deep, the stories unfold.

Glimmers of light dance through the dark,
Each thought ignites a flickering spark.
The muse arrives on gentle wings,
In quiet moments, inspiration springs.

With whispers soft, she stirs the soul,
Awakens visions, makes us whole.
Through brushes, words, and heartfelt breath,
She leaves our fears to fade like death.

In melodies of dusk and dawn,
The noonday sun, the dusk withdrawn.
Creating wonders, stirring pain,
In every heart, a sweet refrain.

With each heartbeat, her song we chase,
In the woven dreams, we find our place.
Forever grateful, we strive to be,
Carriers of her mystery.

Colors of the Mind's Eye

Through the eye of thought, colors blend,
A spectrum bright, no need to mend.
Shades of hope, and hues of fear,
In the mind's eye, they all appear.

Crimson thoughts and azure dreams,
In tangled visions, reality teems.
Luminous ideas break the mold,
A palette forged from stories bold.

Shimmering gold, like laughter's sound,
In silence deep, creativity's found.
Patterns form, narratives rise,
Painting life beneath the skies.

Through vivid brush, we sketch our fate,
In canvas realms, we elevate.
Each stroke a piece of who we are,
A tapestry where hopes are stars.

In the sanctuary of our mind,
All colors merge, their truths aligned.
An artist’s dream, vast and wide,
In the heart of creation, we abide.

The Dance of Creation

In rhythmic pulses, life does sway,
Creating moments, day by day.
Each thought a step, each word a turn,
In every dance, our spirits burn.

With swirling grace, we weave the light,
Crafting shadows that take flight.
A ballet of colors, soft and grand,
Uniting hearts, hand in hand.

From whispers low to thunderous cheers,
Creation's path through laughter, tears.
In every heartbeat, a story flows,
Through the dance, our essence glows.

With open arms, we dare to dream,
In every moment, a sacred stream.
Life's canvas wide, a map to trace,
In the dance of time, we find our place.

So twirl and leap, let spirits soar,
In creation's dance, we seek for more.
With every move, the world ignites,
In this grand ballet, our hearts take flight.

Paths of the Inner Artist

In quiet corners, colors blend,
The inner voice begins to mend.
A brush in hand, the heart takes flight,
Creating worlds shrouded in light.

Dreams weave through shadows and grace,
Every stroke, a sacred space.
Whispers echo, wisdom unfolds,
The artist's tale, timeless and bold.

With every canvas, life is sown,
Through vibrant hues, the self is known.
Textures linger, stories unfurl,
In each creation, a brand new world.

Reflection dances upon the page,
Freedom found, no hint of cage.
To capture essence, to inspire,
Passion ignited, set afire.

So let the spirit soar and roam,
In simple strokes, we find our home.
With open hearts, we boldly start,
Embracing well the inner art.

Surrendering to the Unknown

With gentle breath, we take the leap,
Into the depths, where shadows creep.
The mystery calls, we close our eyes,
To trust in fate, as fear unwinds.

Each moment softens, time unspools,
As knowledge bends and breaks the rules.
In silence found, the answers flow,
Embracing paths we cannot know.

Whispers linger beyond the veil,
In letting go, we hear the tale.
Like autumn leaves that dance away,
We find ourselves in new array.

With open palms, we face the night,
The stars align, the darkness bright.
Surrendering becomes our guide,
A journey vast, no need to hide.

To walk through realms of what could be,
In trust, we find our wild glee.
The unknown beckons, bold and clear,
In every heartbeat, feel the sphere.

Unlocking Boundless Realms

Within the heart, doors gently wait,
To open wide and tempt our fate.
A key of dreams, we hold it tight,
Unlocking worlds, revealing light.

With whispers soft, we turn the lock,
Each click resounds, the spirit shocks.
Beyond the threshold, magic gleams,
Awakening our deepest dreams.

In vibrant colors, visions swirl,
Patterns shift and secrets unfurl.
With every step, new paths align,
In boundless realms, our souls can shine.

Through time and space, we journey far,
Guided by our inner star.
In every heartbeat, echoes sound,
Unlocking realms where love is found.

So take the leap, be unafraid,
In the vastness, dreams are made.
With open hearts, the doors will gleam,
Unlocking life, we find our dream.

The Call of Silent Symbols

In quietude, symbols arise,
They speak to hearts and open eyes.
A language deep, beyond the words,
In every sign, the spirit stirs.

Glimmers shine in shadows cast,
Whispers flutter like leaves amassed.
With ancient lore, they weave the tale,
Of truths concealed, through time we sail.

Each curve and line, a sacred script,
The essence held, the soul equipped.
In patterns etched on earthly ground,
The call of silence, profound and sound.

To listen close, to heed their call,
In stillness found, we grasp it all.
Enigmas light our path ahead,
In silent symbols, dreams are bred.

So follow where the signs appear,
Embrace each story, hold it dear.
In every symbol, let us dive,
To find the magic that's alive.

Chasing Shadows and Light

In twilight's dance, we wander far,
Seeking whispers of a distant star.
Shadows flicker, dreams take flight,
We chase the dusk, embracing night.

Through whispered winds, the secrets flow,
Moments shimmer, ebb and glow.
Light and shadow play their game,
In their embrace, we find our name.

Footsteps soft on the velvet ground,
Echoes linger, a haunting sound.
Paths illuminated, hearts in tune,
Beneath the watchful gaze of the moon.

Each breath a promise, every sigh,
The dance of dreams as time drifts by.
Chasing visions, we run wild,
In the arms of night, forever a child.

From shadows born, to light we flee,
A timeless journey, you and me.
Through every turn, the colors fade,
In the chase of life, memories made.

Fragments of a Fabled Vision

Once in a realm of lore untold,
Where dreams took shape in hues of gold.
Fragments glimmer, stories weave,
In every heart, we dare believe.

In silent woods, a tale unfurls,
Magic dances, as fate swirls.
Echoes linger from ages past,
In time’s embrace, the die is cast.

Wonders hidden in the light,
Fables spark in the dead of night.
Each fragment shines, a guiding star,
Leading us home, no matter how far.

With every breath, the legends grow,
In whispered winds, the secrets flow.
A tapestry of dreams entwined,
In every heart, the hope we find.

So let us chase these shadows bold,
The fragments, tales, and moments told.
In every corner, a treasure lies,
Waiting in silence for our eyes.

Harmonies Beneath the Surface

Beneath the waves, a song takes flight,
Whispers echo in the deep of night.
Harmonies pulse, a hidden art,
In every silence, beats a heart.

Colors swirl, a dance unseen,
Life entwined in shades of green.
Yet in the depths, the stories lie,
Waiting for eyes to glimpse the sky.

With every ripple, secrets call,
Finding solace, we lose our thrall.
The songs of nature softly play,
Guiding travelers on their way.

Through tangled roots, the music flows,
Nature's whispers, where no one goes.
In every note, a truth we seek,
Unveiling wonders, soft and meek.

So dive into the depths profound,
Where harmonies of life surround.
Explore the realms where secrets lie,
And let the ocean's heart reply.

Revelations in Hue

In the dawn of day, colors collide,
Revelations bloom, nowhere to hide.
Each hue a whisper, bold and bright,
Painting the world in soft delight.

Emerald greens brush the glade,
Amber yellows in sunlight played.
Scarlet echoes in twilight's heart,
In every shade, a work of art.

With each sunset, tales unfold,
In fiery tones, the skies behold.
Lavender dreams at the close of day,
Wrapped in hues, we drift away.

In every corner, color ignites,
Sparkling laughter in fading lights.
A canvas stretched across the skies,
In every stroke, the spirit flies.

So let us gather all the shades,
In every heartbeat, the color cascades.
Through every moment, forever new,
Life's beautiful dance in every hue.

Whimsy in Motion

Dancing leaves in the breeze,
Playful whispers of the trees,
Colors blend, a joyful sight,
Nature's canvas, pure delight.

Clouds drift by, a cotton sky,
Children's laughter floating high,
Kites that soar with laughter's cheer,
Whimsy fills the atmosphere.

Waves that crash on sandy shores,
Gulls that dance, their spirits soar,
Footprints drawn in soft, warm sand,
Moments caught, both sweet and grand.

Stars will twinkle, night draws near,
Stories whispered, dreams appear,
In this world of pure emotion,
We find joy in whimsy's motion.

Strokes of Genius

Brush in hand, the canvas waits,
Every stroke, a dance of fates,
Colors clash and then convene,
In the midst, a vibrant scene.

Ideas swirl like paint on white,
Visions born from depths of night,
Whispers turn to art divine,
Inspiration's fleeting line.

Every shadow holds a tale,
In the light, dreams set to sail,
Creating worlds, both bold and bright,
Masterpieces brought to light.

In your heart, the colors blend,
Each creation, a new friend,
With each stroke, a soul refined,
True genius in heart and mind.

A Prism of Possibilities

Rain drops fall as sunlight bends,
Creating colors that transcends,
Shattered light, a moment's grace,
In every hue, a new embrace.

Eyes wide open, dreams take flight,
Paths not traveled, visions bright,
Through the prism, life unfolds,
Stories told, and truths retold.

Hope refracts in every shade,
In this journey, unafraid,
Explorations of the mind,
In the color, peace we find.

From dark to light, we navigate,
In the prism, we create,
Endless choices, wide and free,
A masterpiece of destiny.

Illuminate the Silent

In the quiet, secrets keep,
Whispers dance, where shadows creep,
Calm and still, the world in pause,
Gentle heartbeats, no applause.

Stars above in muted glow,
Guiding paths that few may know,
In silence, truths come alive,
In every breath, the will to strive.

Words unspoken shape the air,
In hidden thoughts, there's beauty rare,
With open minds, we start to see,
The light that thrives, eternally.

Each moment holds a whispered cue,
Illuminating shades of blue,
In the stillness, souls entwine,
Finding light in silent sign.

Unseen Pathways

In shadows deep, we find our way,
Through winding trails where whispers play.
Each step we take, a silent call,
A journey mapped beyond the wall.

With every breath, the night unfolds,
Hidden stories yet untold.
The moonlight dances on the ground,
In unseen pathways, hope is found.

Lost in thought, we wander still,
Chasing dreams, obeying will.
A compass forged of starlit dreams,
Guides our souls like sunlit streams.

The heart's desire, a guiding star,
Leads us forward, near and far.
In silence speaks a wise refrain,
Through unseen pathways, love sustains.

So take my hand, let's tread anew,
In realms of magic, skies so blue.
With courage strong, we'll break the night,
Unseen pathways, pure delight.

Sketches of the Soul

With every brush, the heart reveals,
A canvas shaped by what it feels.
Each stroke a whisper, soft and true,
Sketches of the soul, colored blue.

In shadows cast, the light breaks free,
Painting moments of ecstasy.
Emotions swirl, a vibrant dance,
Sketches of the soul, a fleeting chance.

From darkest hues to brightened shades,
The story of our lives cascades.
With palette rich, we claim our role,
Creating art, sketching the soul.

Layers deep of joy and pain,
Impressions left like gentle rain.
In every grain, a truth reveals,
These sketches hold what time conceals.

So let the colors intertwine,
In morning light, our spirits shine.
With every shape, we find our goal,
In vivid sketches of the soul.

The Palette Within

A treasure trove of hues untold,
The palette whispers, brave and bold.
With every shade, a heartbeat's call,
Layers of life paint over all.

In quiet moments, colors bloom,
Brushing shadows, dispelling gloom.
Each hue a feeling, vivid, bright,
The palette within, a source of light.

From gentle pastels to fiery red,
A symphony of dreams unsaid.
In quiet strokes, we blend and weave,
The palette within, where we believe.

Each color speaks of joy and fear,
Tales of laughter, silent tears.
With open hearts, let's paint our way,
The palette within, come what may.

For every shade we choose to blend,
Reflects the journey, love's true friend.
In vibrant splashes, we shall grow,
The palette within, an endless flow.

Echoes of Imagination

In whispered dreams, the echoes play,
A dance of wonders, night and day.
With every thought, a spark ignites,
Echoes of imagination, taking flight.

A world of colors, vast and deep,
In realms where every secret sleeps.
Each tale unfolds, a twist of fate,
Echoes of imagination, never late.

From distant lands, they softly call,
In vibrant stories that enthrall.
With open minds, we delve beneath,
Echoes of imagination, life bequeath.

A canvas stretched beyond the skies,
Where every dream and hope arise.
With every sigh, we find our spark,
Echoes of imagination, lighting dark.

In silent chambers of the heart,
Where every vision finds its part.
Through whispered paths, our spirits roam,
Echoes of imagination, forever home.

The Dance of the Fractals

In swirling shapes that twist and turn,
Infinite patterns that beckon and yearn,
Each angle whispers secrets untold,
A universe lost, a wonder to behold.

Within the chaos, beauty unfolds,
Symmetries echoing stories of old.
In every curve, a glimpse of the divine,
A fractal dance where numbers align.

From simple seeds, great forests bloom,
In every space, a cosmos resumes.
The light reflects, refracts, and plays,
In fractal realms, time brightly sways.

Like waves on shores, ideas cascade,
Creative forms that never fade.
In the dance of the fractals, we all play,
Embracing the night, welcoming the day.

Lost in the spirals, we twirl and spin,
A journey within, where all begins.
Let the patterns guide us, wild and free,
In the dance of the fractals, just you and me.

Sketches Upon the Breeze

Gentle strokes of wind whisper by,
Carrying dreams that flutter and fly.
Each breath of air a painter's hand,
Sketching stories across the land.

Dancing leaves in autumn's embrace,
Trace fleeting moments, a soft grace.
The laughter of children, echoes so clear,
Capture the essence of joy we hold dear.

Clouds drift lazily across the skies,
Like thoughts that wander, arise and dive.
In the sun's warm glow, shadows blend,
Sketches upon the breeze never end.

Rippling waters reflect the day,
Nature's canvas in vibrant array.
Brushstrokes of color, bold and bright,
Whispers of beauty in soft light.

Beneath the stars, our dreams expand,
Carried gently by the unseen hand.
In every gust, a tale to tell,
Sketches upon the breeze weave a spell.

Embracing the Unconventional

In the margins where few dare to tread,
Lies a world where the wild thoughts spread.
Colors clash, yet harmonize fine,
In the unconventional, true art we find.

Thoughts like rivers meander and flow,
Breaking the molds, daring to grow.
With each step off the beaten path,
We dance in chaos, escaping the math.

Fading echoes of what once was known,
In the silence, new seeds are sown.
Voices that tremble, yet rise up strong,
In embracing the strange, we all belong.

Unraveled threads weave a tale anew,
In the tapestry of dreams, vibrant hue.
Let us paint our lives with brushes bold,
Embracing the stories yet to be told.

Freedom lies where constraints fade,
In the heart of the unconventional made.
Together we'll sing, a raucous refrain,
In the wildest of storms, we'll dance in the rain.

Silent Odes to Creation

In twilight hush, the world breathes slow,
Glimmers of life in the softest glow.
Nature's whispers fill the tranquil air,
Silent odes to creation, a sacred prayer.

Mountains rise in quiet majesty,
Each peak a testament, a mystery.
Rivers carve paths through the stone,
In patience, life finds its own tone.

The stars above take their gentle flight,
Woven in darkness, shimmering bright.
Galaxies swirl in an eternal dance,
A canvas of wonder, a captivating glance.

The heartbeat of earth in rhythmic flow,
Echoes of silence, life's gentle show.
In the quiet moments, we hear the call,
Silent odes to creation, binding us all.

With every dawn, a new tale unfolds,
In the stillness, the universe holds.
Let us listen closely, as dreams take shape,
In silent odes, we find our escape.

Constellations of Creativity

In the night sky, stars collide,
Ideas flicker, side by side.
Dreams are woven, bold and bright,
Guided by the moon's soft light.

Colors swirl in endless dance,
Imagination takes a chance.
Brushstroke whispers fill the air,
Art emerges everywhere.

Shapes and visions intertwine,
In a world where dreams align.
Crafting stories, thoughts unfurl,
Creating magic, boy and girl.

In every line, a spark ignites,
Turning darkness into lights.
Each creation, a new frontier,
A constellation, drawing near.

With every spark, we rise and sing,
Passion flows, creativity's wing.
As we gather, hearts in flight,
We're stardust, painting the night.

Mirrored Reflections

In the glass, a face appears,
Echoing hopes, laughter, fears.
Fragments of the past unfold,
Stories whispered, quietly told.

Each reflection, a fleeting glance,
Moments shared in life's great dance.
In the mirror, truths reside,
Beneath the surface, dreams abide.

Glimmers of joy, shades of pain,
The cycle of losses and gain.
Through the fog, clarity shines,
Guiding paths where life entwines.

In silences, thoughts take root,
From hushed corners, voices shoot.
The mirrored gaze can see it all,
Awakening each muted call.

With every look, we redefine,
Connections deep, our hearts align.
In reflected moments, we find grace,
A tapestry of time and space.

Where Ideas Take Flight

In the mind, where thoughts ignite,
Dreams are born to take their flight.
Wings of vision spread so wide,
Carried on a hopeful tide.

Sparkling notions touch the sky,
Floating freely, soaring high.
Whispers of the winds may guide,
Over valleys far and wide.

With every heartbeat, passions rise,
Creating worlds that mesmerize.
Inventive spirits chase the breeze,
Crafting wonders with such ease.

Ideas twirl like dandelion seeds,
Planting futures from our needs.
Through the clouds, we laugh and play,
Engines of change, we find our way.

Together, we reach for the sun,
Spreading joy, our hearts are one.
In this journey, we take flight,
Exploring dreams both day and night.

The Rhythm of Unspoken Words

In the silence, feelings flow,
Messages only hearts can know.
Echoes dwell in fleeting glance,
A dance of souls, a gentle chance.

With every breath, a story shared,
Quiet hopes, unmasked and bared.
Eyes converse in knowing ways,
Painting truth where silence stays.

A heartbeat whispers, soft and low,
In the space between, we grow.
Unseen ties bind us as one,
Crafting connections, quietly spun.

The rhythm plays a tender tune,
In shrouded light, beneath the moon.
In hidden depths, we find the chords,
A symphony of unspoken words.

Through every pause, the world can feel,
The language spoken is so real.
In still moments, we find the way,
The rhythm of love, come what may.

Glimmers of the Muse

In twilight hues where dreams ignite,
Whispers dance in soft moonlight.
The heartbeats echo, soft and clear,
A symphony only few can hear.

With every stroke, the visions twine,
Colors blend and intertwine.
A muse awakens, bold and bright,
Casting shadows in the night.

Through tangled thoughts, a path unfolds,
Stories whispered, secrets told.
In fleeting moments, truth does shine,
A glimpse of wonder, nearly divine.

Beneath the stars, inspiration flows,
In hidden realms where passion grows.
Each glimmer sparks a radiant fire,
Igniting hope, lifting higher.

So chase the light, embrace the spark,
Dive into the depths, explore the dark.
For in the quiet, magic brews,
In glimmers subtle, life renews.

Daring the Unconventional

With every step that breaks the mold,
A story brave and yet untold.
The road less traveled, rough and wild,
Awakens in the heart of a child.

Against the tide, where others flow,
Adventures wait in realms below.
A spark of chaos, freedom rings,
In the daring, the spirit sings.

To shatter norms, to take the leap,
Into the unknown, secrets keep.
With courage fierce, a path revealed,
In every challenge, truth is yielded.

The winds of change, they howl and race,
Yet in the storm, we find our place.
So raise a glass to journey's quest,
In daring moves, we find our rest.

For every heart that dares to dream,
A universe ignites, agleam.
So let the world see who you are,
In unconventional light, you're a star.

Ascent of the Visionary

In shadows deep where visions grow,
A mind alight begins to flow.
With every thought, the mountains rise,
A vision clear beneath the skies.

To climb beyond the ordinary,
With dreams that swirl, necessary.
Each step unveils a path anew,
As insights spark, the journey's true.

Above the clouds, where eagles soar,
There lies a world we can explore.
With daring heart and widened gaze,
We traverse the fire of brightest blaze.

Through challenges, we carve our way,
In every trial, we learn to sway.
The vision thrives, so rich and bold,
In stories of the dreamers told.

So let the climb be fierce and sweet,
For all who dare refuse defeat.
In ascent true, potential's key,
The visionary sets their spirit free.

The Brush's Secret Language

With strokes so bold, the canvas speaks,
In colors bright, it softly peaks.
Each flick and swirl, a tale untold,
In whispers shared, dreams unfold.

The brush, a wand of artistry,
Creates a world for all to see.
In every shade, emotions flow,
A secret language we all know.

From deep cerulean to softest gold,
The stories told are rich and bold.
With every hue, life finds its way,
In vibrant tones, hearts learn to sway.

Through gentle strokes, the soul is bared,
In silence deep, a promise shared.
The brush speaks truth, both kind and cruel,
A mirror held, revealing jewel.

So let the colors blend and clash,
In every painting, visions thrash.
For in this art, we find our voice,
The brush's language is our choice.

Tides of the Creative Spirit

Waves of thought rush and roam,
Ideas dance like foam.
In the silence, whispers rise,
Born from depths, they touch the skies.

Brush of vision, paint the day,
Brush of longing, fade away.
Every spark ignites the night,
Illuminates with pure delight.

Rippling through the vast unknown,
In the heart, a seed is sown.
Echoes of a mind's embrace,
In each crevice, find a trace.

Tides that ebb and flow like time,
Crafting stories left unchimed.
With each swell, a tale unfolds,
Of dreams and hopes, the spirit holds.

In the rhythm of the sea,
Creation breathes, wild and free.
An endless dance of light and hue,
Awakens life in all we do.

Harmonies of Unspoken Thought

In the hush, a music grows,
Carried on the softest flows.
Notes unplayed in silence wait,
To stir the heart and bend the fate.

Whispers float on gentle air,
A melody crafted with care.
Each moment holds a quiet song,
In the stillness, where we belong.

Eyes that meet speak volumes clear,
A language felt, yet never here.
In shadows cast, we find a tune,
Eclipsed by night, kissed by the moon.

Threads of connection, softly spun,
Bind our souls, two into one.
In the depth of unshared dreams,
There lies a world bursting at the seams.

Harmony rises, slowly unfolds,
In the silence, truth beholds.
A gentle breath, a knowing glance,
In this space, we find our chance.

Fragments of a Fleeting Dream

Shattered pieces of the night,
Woven in soft, silver light.
Glimmers lost like morning dew,
Fading fast, yet holding true.

In the corners of the mind,
Visions dance, yet hard to bind.
Echoes whisper tales unsaid,
In the labyrinths of the head.

Colors melt in twilight's sigh,
Like fleeting moments passing by.
Grab them close, then let them fly,
In the warmth of dreams, we lie.

Flashes spark, then disappear,
Leaving only the sweet veneer.
In their wake, we long and yearn,
For the lessons we must learn.

Bow to the fragile nature’s art,
Where dreams begin and often part.
In the fleeting, find the gold,
Stories yet to be retold.

The Alchemy of Emotion

In the crucible of the heart,
Feelings meld, each a part.
Heat from passion, cool from doubt,
Transforming all, within, without.

Mystic blends of joy and pain,
Crafting gold from the mundane.
A touch of sorrow, a dash of glee,
In this mix, we find the key.

Depths of love, the strength of fear,
Elixirs brewed from what we hold dear.
In the alchemy of our days,
Emerging truths obscure the haze.

Brewing storms in tranquil streams,
Potions brewed from shattered dreams.
Each emotion, a vibrant hue,
Painting life in shades anew.

Embrace this art, let it flow,
For within us, wonders grow.
In the melding, we transcend,
To find the gold that love can send.

Shards of a Dreamscape

In twilight's grasp, shadows confide,
Whispers of wishes in silence reside.
Fragments of memory, dancing in night,
Lost in the echoes, yet seeking the light.

Colors that bleed on a canvas of air,
Twisting through time with the weight of despair.
A tapestry woven from hopes yet unspoken,
Promises linger, yet hearts remain broken.

Mirrors reflect what the soul can embrace,
Shards of a dreamscape, a fractured space.
Fleeting desires melt under the moon,
Each glimmer a note in a haunting tune.

Through portals of slumber, we wander afar,
Finding our visions—each heart a rare star.
In dreams we discover what fate seeks to find,
The shards of our spirit, entwined and aligned.

The Unfolding Canvas

A brush in hand, the colors ignite,
Each stroke a heartbeat, a dance with delight.
On the canvas of life, stories unfold,
In vivid embraces, the brave and the bold.

Layers of whispers, entwined in the haze,
Shadows of moments, both fragile and brave.
With every new shade, a memory blooms,
Painting the silence with vibrant costumes.

In the chatter of hues, a symphony plays,
Creating a world where the spirit sways.
Fingers like raindrops, they trail down the line,
Connecting each thought with a rhythm divine.

Each canvas inviting a tale yet unsung,
A testament crafted by hearts that are young.
As colors collide, we embrace what we see,
In the unfolding canvas, we find purity.

The Pulse of Creation

From whispers of dust, a spark takes to flight,
In the silence of dawn, where dreams chase the light.
The pulse of creation, a rhythm divine,
Beating in unison, yours, and mine.

The cosmos, a canvas, where galaxies merge,
Each flicker, a heartbeat, a ceaseless surge.
Atoms colliding, a symphony's birth,
From chaos to order, we cherish our worth.

With every new dawn, the circle begins,
Awakening life where the journey spins.
Hands reach to the heavens, embracing the fire,
Building our dreams with fervent desire.

Within every heartbeat, a song waits to rise,
A testament vibrant, constellations in skies.
The pulse of creation—the essence we share,
A tapestry woven with infinite care.

Serendipity in Strokes

In a world of serendipity, colors collide,
Brush strokes unravel where secrets reside.
Hidden treasures in every embrace,
Artistry blooming, a sacred space.

Paint spills and ripples, a dance unforeseen,
Magic unwinds in the spaces between.
Each whimsical line, a twist of the fate,
Creating a story we bravely create.

With laughter like bubbles, our hearts intertwine,
Crafting connections in patterns divine.
Every mistake, a chance to evolve,
In serendipity's arms, all dreams will resolve.

The beauty of chaos, the joy of the free,
In strokes we discover our true destiny.
As colors converge, a masterpiece grows,
In the dance of existence, our wonder bestows.

The Enigma of Expression

Whispers of the soul unfold,
In colors bright, in tales untold.
A dance of thoughts in silent streams,
Where shadows linger, and hope redeems.

Each stroke a voice, each hue a tale,
As dreams take flight on a fragile gale.
Emotions spill from canvas bare,
A journey woven with tender care.

The heart's enigma, a mystery wide,
In layers deep where secrets hide.
Bold strokes clash, then softly blend,
A story crafted that knows no end.

Through chaos, calm emerges clear,
In every dip, a sigh, a fear.
Mirrored feelings, dark and light,
Painting whispers through the night.

In artistry, the truth does lie,
A bond of silence, a hopeful cry.
Unraveled joy, embraced in pain,
The enigma lives in heart's domain.

Revelations in Color

In every hue, a world unfolds,
Stories breathing, warm or cold.
Painted moments, rich and bright,
Revelations dance in morning light.

Crimson dreams and azure skies,
Brushstrokes whisper, where mystery lies.
Emerald echoes and golden gleam,
Life revealed in a visual dream.

Against the canvas, shadows play,
A palette kisses night and day.
From muted depths to vibrant peaks,
In silence, beauty gently speaks.

Textures merge, sensations rise,
The heart composes, through every guise.
In swirls and strokes, new visions bloom,
Infinite tales of light and gloom.

With every canvas, hope ignites,
In every corner, color fights.
Revealing layers, pure and true,
Revelations born anew in hue.

The Symphony of Brush and Ink

A symphony of ink and brush,
In quiet corners, colors rush.
Harmonies of thought align,
Where artistry's heart begins to shine.

Notes of contrast, strokes reveal,
The liquid dance of what we feel.
Each line a note in vibrant song,
Together they create, they belong.

In shadows cast, a melody,
A rhythm forms a symphony.
The paper sighs, the canvas breathes,
In every stroke, a heart believes.

Echoes rise in layered depths,
Expressed in art, the soul's own steps.
A crescendo born from silence bare,
Where moments linger, free from care.

The brush waltzes, ink unfolds,
As stories gather, dreams take hold.
With every stroke, a sweet refrain,
The symphony of art remains.

Shadows Converge

In twilight's grasp, the shadows meet,
Whispers linger on silent street.
Shapes entwine in dusky glow,
Secrets hidden, tales bestow.

They dance along where light retreats,
In corners dark, where silence greets.
A gentle hush, a fleeting glance,
Where echoes linger, shadows dance.

Beneath the moon's soft, watchful eye,
The night unveils what dreams imply.
Figures blend in shades of gray,
As lingering thoughts begin to sway.

Unraveled truths in darkness found,
In quiet moments, hearts unbound.
As shadows converge, the soul takes flight,
In whispered secrets and fading light.

With every shadow, stories glean,
A tapestry woven, unseen.
In the stillness, the heart may learn,
That shadows speak, and brightly burn.

Unveiling the Inner Vision

In silence deep, the mind takes flight,
Awakening dreams in the soft moonlight.
A canvas waits for whispers pure,
To paint the heart, a vision sure.

Each thought a brush, each sigh a stroke,
In the quiet, fierce hopes provoke.
A landscape vast, where shadows blend,
With colors bright, the echoes send.

Glimmers of truth in the twilight gleam,
Unraveled tales in an endless dream.
Each moment caught, a treasure found,
In the stillest air, the soul unbound.

Awaken, spirit, let the light flow,
In the depths of you, let wisdom grow.
A journey profound, to realms unknown,
Where visions thrive, and fears are sown.

With every breath, let colors rise,
In the heart's embrace, the soul complies.
An inner world, vast and free,
Unveiling the truth of what will be.

Chasing Shadows of Creation

In the quiet dark, where dreams ignite,
Shadows dance in the pale starlight.
A thrill unfolds, in silence profound,
Chasing whispers, a melody found.

The pulse of time, a gentle sway,
Guiding hearts to the break of day.
In each flicker, a story untold,
The light emerges from the bold.

Moments collide, in a cosmic spin,
Chasing the echoes, where dreams begin.
A rhythm beats, an ancient song,
In harmony deep, where we belong.

Colors swirl, as shadows play,
Mingling softly in a bright ballet.
The heart ignites with visions loud,
In the chaos, we stand proud.

Chasing shadows, we find our way,
In the dawn of hope, the night gives way.
With every step, creation flows,
In the depths of us, a universe grows.

The Dance of Inspiration

In the morning light, a soft caress,
Inspiration blooms, a wilderness.
With every step, we chase the muse,
In the flowing rhythm, we must choose.

On whispered winds, ideas soar,
Painting the skies, forevermore.
The cadence calls, a vibrant song,
In the dance of light, we all belong.

Moments flutter, like leaves in air,
Captured softly, beyond compare.
The heart leaps high, with dreams to share,
In every beat, the universe bare.

With laughter light, and shadows deep,
Awake our souls, the fire to keep.
A flicker bright, a guiding flame,
In the dance of life, we forge our name.

Inspiration throb, like a wild stream,
Flowing freely, in the heart's gleam.
Together twirling, we rise and spin,
In the art of life, we find within.

Colors Whisper Secrets

In the garden of hues, where petals play,
Colors whisper secrets of the day.
In vibrant strokes, the world unveils,
In every shade, a story sails.

The red of passion, a fiery spark,
Blue like the sea, where dreams embark.
Golden sunbeams weave through leaves,
In the palette of life, the heart believes.

Each hue a note in a symphony bright,
Painting the canvas, morning to night.
In the quiet hum, the colors blend,
Whispering stories that never end.

Through shadows soft, and light's embrace,
Colors reveal a hidden grace.
In their language, a promise sings,
In the heart of all, the beauty clings.

A tapestry of life, so richly spun,
In the dance of colors, we are one.
Listen closely, let your heart soar,
For in their whispers, we find much more.

The Pulse of Creation

In shadows deep, the spark ignites,
Where silence breathes, the heart delights.
With every beat, a vision flows,
From chaos grand, the beauty grows.

A dance of light in midnight's veil,
Unraveled threads tell every tale.
Each note a whisper, soft yet loud,
The pulse of life, a vibrant crowd.

In nature’s grasp, the colors blend,
With every turn, the cycles fend.
A canvas bright, where dreams take flight,
The rhythm sways in endless night.

Through every storm, the stillness waits,
As time a canvas, love palates.
Creation blooms in fleeting breath,
Eternal dance of life and death.

With every stroke, the world ignites,
In visions bold, our spirit fights.
The pulse of creation sings its song,
In this great symphony, we all belong.

Celestial Patterns

Stars entwined in cosmic thread,
Mapping paths of those long fled.
A tapestry of time and space,
In stillness found, we seek our place.

Galaxies swirl in midnight glow,
Whispers of secrets, long ago.
In constellations, stories weave,
Celestial patterns, hard to believe.

Nebula's hues paint skies anew,
Each hue a moment, rich and true.
Through endless voids, the light will speak,
In silence vast, we learn to seek.

A comet's trail, a fleeting spark,
Illuminates the cold and dark.
In cosmic dance, we find our song,
To the rhythm of the stars, we belong.

Eclipses pass, the shadows wane,
In cycles bound, we find our gain.
Each twinkling light a guide above,
Celestial patterns wrap us in love.

Explorations Beyond the Canvas

With brush in hand, a world unfolds,
In vivid strokes, the heart beholds.
Beyond the frame, horizons call,
Adventures sought in vast expanse.

Colors clash in wild delight,
As dreams collide, both day and night.
Each layer thick with whispered fears,
In every hue, the world appears.

Textures breathe, alive and real,
In art, the truths, our hearts reveal.
With every stroke, we break the mold,
To seek the stories yet untold.

Shadows dance in corners wide,
Where light and dark become our guide.
Explorations that ignite the soul,
Through vivid tales, we become whole.

In every piece, a piece of heart,
Through brush and ink, we play our part.
Beyond the canvas, we dare to dream,
In endless realms, where passions gleam.

Muse in the Moonlight

Beneath the glow of silver beams,
The night awakens softest dreams.
A muse appears in gentle light,
In whispered secrets of the night.

With every glance, the shadows play,
The heart ignites, the mind will sway.
In moonlit dance, our souls align,
A magic spell, the stars entwine.

In quiet places, thoughts take flight,
A canvas filled with pure delight.
From distant shores, we hear the call,
Of every wish that seeks to fall.

With every heart beat, stories bloom,
Echoes of love, dispelling gloom.
In the still air where silence thrives,
The muse in moonlight softly drives.

As dawn approaches, shadows fade,
Yet memories linger, unafraid.
In twilight's hush, we find our way,
The muse remains, come what may.